God of Many Faces

Margaret Renshaw FMA

© Margaret Renshaw

Don Bosco Publications
Thornleigh House
Bolton BL1 6PQ
Tel: 01204 308 811
Fax: 01204 306 868

www.salesians.org.uk

ISBN 0-9544539-2-1

printed by
The Catholic Printing Company of Farnworth
35 Oxford Road, Altrincham,
Cheshire WA14 2ED.
Telephone: 0161 929 9633 Fax: 0161 926 9032
E mail: enquiries@catholicprintco.co.uk

Contents

Introduction

Living in the Lake District is a never-ending source of joy. Here, in its beauty, no matter what the season, there is a sense of God, of something infinitely great, of something beyond ourselves. There is an awesomeness in the majesty of the mountains, in the ever-changing colour of sky and water, in the peace and mystery of the lakes, in the patchwork of green fields dotted with sheep and cattle. Wild flowers grow in profusion, painting the meadows with every shade of colour.

Many years ago the psalmist said exultantly,
I marvel at the wonder of my being.
We too, are beautiful, we are made by God and are precious in His sight. In the beauty of ourselves we are drawn into the beauty of God.
Is it beauty that entrances us?
Or could it be –
The One who made the beauty
Tugging at our heart,
In the loveliness we see?

All beauty should bring us nearer to God, should bring us back to the Divine within us. These simple reflections are about you and me, about God's creation in all its forms, about the beauty and majesty of God Himself.

Margaret Renshaw FMA

Parents

How beautiful they are
In the autumn of their days.
White hair and wrinkled hands
Show the passing of the years.
Love and pain have made them strong,
Have bound them both together,
Given them hearts which overflow
With graciousness and blessing.
Love enshrines their sorrow.
Each new day, as it comes along,
Heralds a glad tomorrow.
We, your children, salute you
For the life you brought to birth.
Your love, your care, your sacrifice
Blessed those early years on earth.

When I ask God's blessing on you,
I am asking for His love to be poured upon you.
His energy and strength to rest
On you who are now blessed.
Blessing of love to encircle you,
Touch of His hand to heal.
Through life His presence with you,
His challenge to reveal.
So dear friend, I gladly say,
God bless you.

Memories

No matter where I am,
No matter what I be,
I know I carry with me –
My treasured memories.

Remembering joys and pain,
They bring tears to my eyes.
Remembering the love of friends,
The sadness of goodbyes.

So much I remember.
All the loveliness of life
I see now in my pain,
Woven strands of light.

Strands return in memory
To chase away dark night.
God's gift of memory
Giving me new sight.

Unfailing love and care
You have always given me,
Sharing in my laughter,
Walking troubled ways with me.

Supporting hand outstretched,
Gift given generously,
When you said at the supper,
'Do this in my memory'.

Beauty

Beauty has such power on us,
We must stand and stare.
Gently it uplifts us
Into another sphere.

A sphere all innocence,
Peace and purity.
We clearly sense
Love's priority.

A call back to beauty
Sounds within our soul,
Spirit of God within us,
A divinity to own.

Beauty brings us back to God,
Soul and beauty resonate.
God of all loveliness,
Beauty incarnate.

Is it beauty that entrances us?
Or could it be –
The One who made the beauty
Tugging at our heart,
In the loveliness we see?

Why?

Why do we feel we must always move,
Always be on the go?
Why can't we sit and look about
And watch the flowers grow?
Why can't we look at the Autumn leaves
Turning scarlet, yellow and brown?
Turning and twirling in a dervish dance,
Then tired, they must lie down.
Why can't we look at the sunset
Bathe in its radiant glow?
Colours no artist can create
Are ours if we did but know.
Why can't we see birds on the wing
Soar and float in the air
Free as the clouds drifting above?
Why can't we stand and stare?
We fill our days with work and worry,
And so we cannot see
All the many beautiful things
Created for you and me.

Each moment is God's gift to me,
If I use it well in love,
It becomes my gift to God.

Meadow Flowers in Spring

After the aconite has lavished gold,
And the snowdrop shed her tears,
Anemone, the windflower, then appears.

Anemone, winsome flower of Spring,
Delicate, white, you sigh in the breeze,
Adding your song to whispering trees.

Feast of beauty you bring to our fields
Tremulous flower, leaves tender green,
Friend of the primrose and gold celandine.

With faces wide open you gaze at the sun.
Carpets of colour you weave on our fields.
Your beauty covers the meadows.

Your care and loveliness, my Lord,
Shines in the beauty of the earth,
Your smile in each flower's birth.

The way ahead is an open road,
Full of vision and promise.
Don't look back at what is past,
Walk the new road with Christ.

The Shell

I held a shell to my ear,
Heard the ocean pounding.
From far away I could hear
The angry waves resounding.

Was this a history of my past,
An echo of my feelings,
Of the blows handed out to me,
Of sadness at life's dealings?

I held a shell to my ear,
I heard a gentle swishing,
The hush of peaceful ocean waves
That made the heart-beat listen.

Was this again a part of my past,
Of all the love I'd been given,
The gentleness and peacefulness
That made our home a haven?

O shell, you whispered in my ear
Stories of love and pain.
Together they've made me what I am,
A child of the sun and gale.

A child that basks in the love of the Son,
Accepts the challenge He brings.
Will harmonise the sorrows and the joys
And thro' them all will sing.

The Roe Deer

It was a sullen, misty day,
Rain hanging in the air,
The shrouded world was grey.

Suddenly from out the darkness
A roe deer leapt in play,
Epitome of joy and gladness.

In a moment it was gone
But its beauty stayed,
Turning a grey day into song.

What sight so peaceful as the unturned earth,
What strength lies hidden there,
Germ of life, awaiting birth.
Fields lying brown in sun and rain,
Hold the stirrings of life.
Life that will flower into golden grain,
Into wheat become the bread of life.
Wheat become the Body of Christ.

Death

What is death? It is that I shall see
The Christ who, invisible, walked this earth with me.

The one who loved and cherished me from birth
Now has come to take me from this earth.

I'll feel His arms around me, in loving care
Taking me home where I shall breathe God's air.

In awe I'll gaze at pierced hands and feet,
Life now divine and wondrous sweet.

My Lord, death is to be at one with Thee,
All Thy glory and Thy joy to see,
I forever worshipping and loving Thee.

Somewhere below low clouds
Came a seagull's lonely cry.
Above a solitary buzzard mewed and cried.
Across the sodden grass
Shadows lay dark and deep.
Nature moaned in sleep and softly cried.
Here my cottage fire crackles in the grate,
Walls reflect the flame, I'm warm and safe.

The Gale and Me

Today I went into a gale,
The wind pushed and chivvied me,
Screamed in my ear, tore at my clothes.
Was this wind-tossed person really me?
Gone all sense of poise and power,
I felt no longer free,
Taken into an invisible world
That no longer belonged to me.
My secure little world had disappeared
In the wildness of wind and rain,
Yet I felt an affinity to the cry of the wild
To the screeching of its pain.
Perhaps there's a wildness in all of us
That needs to be set free.
To shout and laugh at life's vagaries
To find the inner me.
To struggle with storm, wind and rain,
To find meaning in life,
Yet know at the very heart of the storm
Lies the heart of the risen Christ.

Every experience in our lives
Is like a seed, planted within us.
Nurture this seed,
For it will become something strong
That will sustain us, challenge us,
Open our eyes to a world newly born.

Reverence

We walk the earth in beauty,
In the beauty of this mortal life.
The divine lies deep within us
Breathing an aura of light.

We call on this sacred place
For a reverence of all that be.
For soil gives life to earth's face,
To the glorious wonder of me.

I never will know fully
The miracle of all I see.
The wonder of God's creation
Remains a mystery.

Mystery of love's outpouring,
Drawing us to praise.
Uniting all people together
In love of His wondrous ways.

Love has a way of travelling around.
I go out and give it, when I come back,
She's sitting in my chair, smiling at me.

Blue Butterfly

Your chrysalis cracks and opens wide,
As you struggle to appear,
Arrayed in dress of sapphire blue,
Dainty creature of sun and air.
You caught your colour from the sky
And brought it down to earth,
With it came the shining sun
Rejoicing at your birth.
You float from flower to flower,
Fluttering in the air,
Blue speck, a gift from heaven
So soon to disappear.

We are wounded, hurt,
Hurt beyond all grieving.
Only the touch of His hand
Will bring us healing.

God of Many Faces

His face is everywhere.
In the smallest flower,
In the mightiest tree,
In the surge of ocean.
In the flight of the bee,
In the sun's glorious setting,
In dawn's gentle rise,
In lake water fretting,
As it gently sighs.
In the wildness of youth,
In the peace of the old,
In mother's eyes smiling,
As she looks at her child.
In little ones gurgling,
With joy of new life.
In the kiss of forgiveness
Ending all strife.
At times His face
Full of light and peace,
At other times veiled
In lines of grief.
Today I found his face
In the stale sweat of a beggar
Who came to my door.

Trust is a leap into the unknown,
Knowing that there in the darkness,
Arms of God to hold me,
I will never be left alone.

Beautiful Bird

They gave me a lump of clay,
Make something of it they said.
I sat for a while and thought,
I'll make a beautiful bird.

Poor bird, wings flopping,
Legs were all askew,
Head dangerously wobbling,
Feathers far too few.

They laughed, but I loved it,
Loved every misshapen part.
Even loved the squint in its eye
The beak that was coming apart.

God looks at what I've made of me.
Well-meaning, but blundering me.
Sees weakness, foibles and failings,
Through it all, He's loving me.

He created me, I am His.

Father, you are the potter, I am the clay,
The work of your hands.
(Isaiah)

The Journey

I journey each day,
Not knowing what the day has in store.
One certainty I have,
I could not, would not, ask for more.
For you walk with me
Along life's oft-troubled way.

As I journey on
Each dark night and luminous day,
On Thee I lean.
When the winding road to Heaven seems
long
You give me energy,
And strength and love to carry on.

When the journey's done,
My wandering feet now still,
I'll radiantly see,
The love, the glory, the majesty
Surrounding Thee.

The light of Resurrection
Shines in the darkness of the cross,
Through the suffering of the world,
In the grief, the pain, the loss,
We can be transfigured
By the power of His cross.

The Fire in the Hearth

From the white heart of the fire,
Red flames leap up high.
Crackling, sparkling, pulsating with life,
They flare, leap up and die.
Other flames take up the dance,
Pirouetting in rainbow hue.
Stretching their arms to the darkness above,
Before glowing low to gently die.
All that is left of the beauty and glow,
Is the warmth in a heap of grey ash.
Yet here in its heart there lies a spark
That, with a breath, will come to life.

In the grey ashes of my heart,
God sees a spark of light.
His spirit gently breathes on it,
I come again to life.
Life that treasures God's spirit within,
That leaps up in joyful praise.
Alive to the Spirit working in me,
I dance in the warmth of His flame.

By the beauty of their presence,
By their love unfailing,
Friends, God's gift to us
Is one of His greatest blessings.

Life

We begin, we end.
What goes on in between?
So much of life to be garnered,
So much to see and feel.

Life comes with open hands to us,
It holds our hopes and fears.
The frustration and the hassle,
The laughter, the joys and tears.

We all carry wounds, we are all scarred,
But have joy to balance the pain.
Each new experience makes us grow,
As dry grass after rain.

The greatest gift life has given
Is the God-blessed gift of love.
It helps us walk our pilgrim way,
Back to the source of love.

Who can know what suffering is?
Who can probe its power?
A power that takes me in the dark
And makes of me a coward.
It's up to us. Negate that power!
Be brave in the face of pain,
To realise we're lifted up,
If we give God our pain.

Hope

Hope is a beautiful lady
Eyes gleam with light,
Radiance beams from her
Even in darkest night.

She smiles from the face of the newly born,
From the burgeoning trees and ripening corn.
She enters the cracks of the most hardened heart,
Shedding her light, dispelling the dark.

She goes straight to the place where the wound lies,
Lays balm on the pain of blackened waste.
Releases the despair where the spirit cries,
Opens shut doors for the coming grace.

O hope, our comforter and joy,
Shining light piercing dark night.
Walk with us as we journey on
To God and the eternal light.

Daisies open their golden eyes
And smile at the rising sun,
Smile, as they have always smiled,
Since the world has begun.